LIFE IS A
JOURNEY
NOT A
DESTINATION

summersdale

LIFE IS A JOURNEY, NOT A DESTINATION

Summersdale Publishers Ltd
46 West Street
Chichester
West Sussex
PO19 1RP
UK

www.summersdale.com

Printed and bound in the Czech Republic

ISBN: 978-1-84953-821-3

Substantial discounts on bulk quantities of Summersdale books are available to corporations, professional associations and other organisations. For details contact general enquiries: telephone: +44 (0) 1243 771107, fax: +44 (0) 1243 786300 or email: enquiries@summersdale.com

TO **AISTE**

FROM **ANDRÉA**

YOU ARE NEVER TOO
OLD TO SET ANOTHER
GOAL OR TO DREAM
A NEW DREAM.

Les Brown

HITCH YOUR
WAGON TO A STAR.

Ralph Waldo Emerson

IN ORDER TO CARRY A
POSITIVE ACTION WE
MUST DEVELOP HERE
A POSITIVE VISION.

Dalai Lama

DON'T JUST DREAM IT... LIVE IT!

ANYONE WHO HAS
NEVER MADE A MISTAKE
HAS NEVER TRIED
ANYTHING NEW.

Albert Einstein

EVERYTHING THAT IS
DONE IN THE WORLD
IS DONE BY HOPE.

Martin Luther

BE A GOAL
DIGGER

A HEAD FULL OF
DREAMS HAS NO
SPACE FOR FEARS.

Anonymous

YOU ONLY LIVE ONCE,
BUT IF YOU DO IT RIGHT,
ONCE IS ENOUGH.

Mae West

THE MAN ON TOP OF THE MOUNTAIN DIDN'T FALL THERE.

Vince Lombardi

NO ONE KNOWS
WHAT HE CAN DO
TILL HE TRIES.

Publilius Syrus

MAKE
YOUR OWN
SUNSHINE

ONE DOESN'T DISCOVER
NEW LANDS WITHOUT
CONSENTING TO LOSE
SIGHT, FOR A VERY LONG
TIME, OF THE SHORE.

André Gide

IF YOU WANT TO ACHIEVE GREATNESS, STOP ASKING FOR PERMISSION.

Anonymous

LIVE
FOR
TODAY

ALL GREAT
ACHIEVEMENTS
REQUIRE TIME.

David J. Schwartz

WE ARE ALL IN THE
GUTTER, BUT SOME
OF US ARE LOOKING
AT THE STARS.

Oscar Wilde

ALL LIFE IS AN
EXPERIMENT. THE MORE
EXPERIMENTS YOU
MAKE THE BETTER.

Ralph Waldo Emerson

THE BRAVE MAN IS NOT
HE WHO DOES NOT FEEL
AFRAID, BUT HE WHO
CONQUERS THAT FEAR.

Nelson Mandela

BE SO GOOD
THEY CAN'T
IGNORE
YOU

A JOURNEY OF A THOUSAND MILES BEGINS WITH A SINGLE STEP.

Lao Tzu

STUDY AS IF YOU WERE
TO LIVE FOREVER.
LIVE AS IF YOU WERE
TO DIE TOMORROW.

Isidore of Seville

YOU'VE GOT
TO START
SOMEWHERE

THE VISION MUST BE FOLLOWED BY THE VENTURE.

Vance Havner

IF IT SCARES YOU,
IT MIGHT BE A GOOD
THING TO TRY.

Seth Godin

YOU MUST BE THE
CHANGE YOU WISH TO
SEE IN THE WORLD.

Mahatma Gandhi

DIFFICULT ROADS OFTEN LEAD TO BEAUTIFUL DESTINATIONS.

Melchor Lim

BE A WARRIOR,
NOT A WORRIER

HE THAT WAITS UPON
FORTUNE, IS NEVER
SURE OF A DINNER.

Benjamin Franklin

LIFE ISN'T ABOUT
FINDING YOURSELF;
IT'S ABOUT CREATING
YOURSELF.

George Bernard Shaw

ALWAYS
BELIEVE THAT
SOMETHING
WONDERFUL
IS ABOUT TO
HAPPEN

NO ONE CAN
MAKE YOU FEEL
INFERIOR WITHOUT
YOUR CONSENT.

Eleanor Roosevelt

GREATNESS IS MORE
THAN POTENTIAL. IT
IS THE EXECUTION OF
THAT POTENTIAL.

Eric Burns

THE FIRST STEP
BINDS ONE TO
THE SECOND.

French proverb

IN THE END, WE ONLY
REGRET THE CHANCES
WE DIDN'T TAKE.

Anonymous

LIVE FOR THE
MOMENTS YOU
CAN'T PUT
INTO WORDS

THROW OFF THE
BOWLINES. SAIL AWAY
FROM THE SAFE
HARBOUR. CATCH
THE TRADE WINDS IN
YOUR SAILS. EXPLORE.
DREAM. DISCOVER.

H. Jackson Brown Jr

LIFE BEGINS AT THE END OF YOUR COMFORT ZONE.

Neale Donald Walsch

ENJOY
THE LITTLE
THINGS

NOT ALL THOSE WHO WANDER ARE LOST.

J. R. R. Tolkien

FIRST SAY TO YOURSELF
WHAT YOU WOULD BE;
AND THEN DO WHAT
YOU HAVE TO DO.

Epictetus

THERE IS AN HOUR
IN EACH MAN'S LIFE
APPOINTED TO MAKE
HIS HAPPINESS, IF
THEN HE SEIZE IT.

Beaumont and Fletcher

LIFE IS EITHER A DARING ADVENTURE OR NOTHING.

Helen Keller

DON'T SAVE YOUR
DREAMS FOR
YOUR SLEEP

LIFE IS LIKE RIDING
A BICYCLE. TO KEEP
YOUR BALANCE YOU
MUST KEEP MOVING.

Albert Einstein

MAY YOU LIVE
ALL THE DAYS OF
YOUR LIFE.

Jonathan Swift

MAKE
EVERY
MINUTE
COUNT

IF YOU CAN DREAM IT,
YOU CAN DO IT.

Tom Fitzgerald

FORGET PAST
MISTAKES. FORGET
FAILURES. FORGET
EVERYTHING EXCEPT
WHAT YOU'RE GOING
TO DO NOW AND DO IT.

William Durant

THE GARDEN OF THE
WORLD HAS NO LIMITS,
EXCEPT IN YOUR MIND.

Rumi

PERSEVERANCE IS
FAILING NINETEEN
TIMES AND SUCCEEDING
THE TWENTIETH.

Julie Andrews

THE EXPERIENCE, NOT THE END POINT, IS THE REWARD

BE THE BEST VERSION OF YOU.

Anonymous

KIND WORDS
WILL UNLOCK AN
IRON DOOR.

Turkish proverb

LIVE
EVERY DAY AS
IF IT WERE
YOUR LAST

ANYONE WHO LIVES
WITHIN THEIR MEANS
SUFFERS FROM A LACK
OF IMAGINATION.

Oscar Wilde

YOUR LIFE DOES
NOT GET BETTER
BY CHANCE, IT GETS
BETTER BY CHANGE.

Jim Rohn

WE ARE THE CHANGE THAT WE SEEK.

Barack Obama

YOU HAVE TO GO OUT
THERE AND MAKE
YOUR OWN MISTAKES
IN ORDER TO LEARN.

Emma Watson

TAKE ON
TODAY'S
CHALLENGES

LIFE ISN'T A MATTER OF MILESTONES, BUT OF MOMENTS.

Rose Kennedy

A NEGATIVE MIND
WILL NEVER GIVE YOU
A POSITIVE LIFE.

Anonymous

DO
SOMETHING
NEW EVERY
DAY

LET YOUR SMILE
CHANGE THE WORLD, BUT
DON'T LET THE WORLD
CHANGE YOUR SMILE.

Anonymous

A LIFE SPENT MAKING
MISTAKES IS NOT ONLY
MORE HONOURABLE,
BUT MORE USEFUL
THAN A LIFE SPENT
DOING NOTHING.

George Bernard Shaw

BEGIN WHATEVER
YOU HAVE TO DO: THE
BEGINNING OF A WORK
STANDS FOR THE WHOLE.

Ausonius

THE TRICK IS TO ENJOY
LIFE. DON'T WISH AWAY
YOUR DAYS, WAITING FOR
BETTER ONES AHEAD.

Marjorie Pay Hinckley

DON'T JUST
RACE FOR THE
FINISH LINE

YOU HAVEN'T FAILED UNTIL YOU QUIT TRYING.

Anonymous

OPPORTUNITIES
MULTIPLY AS THEY
ARE SEIZED.

Sun Tzu

LIFE ISN'T
A DRESS
REHEARSAL;
GRAB IT WHILE
YOU CAN

IT IS TODAY THAT WE
MUST CREATE THE
WORLD OF THE FUTURE.

Eleanor Roosevelt

FAILURE IS SIMPLY
THE OPPORTUNITY TO
BEGIN AGAIN, THIS TIME
MORE INTELLIGENTLY.

Henry Ford

LIFE IS TO BE ENJOYED, NOT JUST ENDURED.

Gordon B. Hinckley

TO THOSE WHO CAN
DREAM, THERE IS
NO SUCH PLACE
AS FAR AWAY.

Anonymous

LIVE
SIMPLY,
DREAM
BIG

IF WE WERE MEANT
TO STAY IN ONE PLACE,
WE'D HAVE ROOTS
INSTEAD OF FEET.

Rachel Wolchin

SUCCESS IS OFTEN
ACHIEVED BY THOSE
WHO DON'T KNOW THAT
FAILURE IS INEVITABLE.

Coco Chanel

WHAT ARE
YOU WAITING
FOR?

THE HARDER THE
CONFLICT, THE MORE
GLORIOUS THE TRIUMPH.

Thomas Paine

NOTHING THAT IS
CAN PAUSE OR STAY;
THE MOON WILL WAX,
THE MOON WILL WANE,
THE MIST AND CLOUD
WILL TURN TO RAIN,
THE RAIN TO MIST
AND CLOUD AGAIN,
TOMORROW BE TODAY.

Henry Wadsworth Longfellow

LIFE IS BETTER WHEN YOU'RE LAUGHING.

Anonymous

SET YOUR GOALS HIGH,
AND DON'T STOP TILL
YOU GET THERE.

Bo Jackson

USE THE
NEGATIVES TO
MAKE A BETTER
PICTURE

TRY TO BE A RAINBOW IN SOMEONE'S CLOUD.

Maya Angelou

I AM NOT A PRODUCT
OF MY CIRCUMSTANCES.
I AM A PRODUCT OF
MY DECISIONS.

Stephen Covey

NEVER
GIVE UP
YOUR CHILDISH
PLEASURES

IF YOU DON'T BUILD
YOUR OWN DREAM,
SOMEBODY WILL
HIRE YOU TO HELP
BUILD THEIRS.

Tony A. Gaskins Jr

THERE ARE SO
MANY THINGS THAT
WE WISH WE HAD
DONE YESTERDAY.

Mignon McLaughlin

MISTAKES ARE PROOF
THAT YOU'RE TRYING.

Anonymous

AS WE LET OUR OWN
LIGHT SHINE, WE
UNCONSCIOUSLY GIVE
OTHERS PERMISSION
TO DO THE SAME.

Marianne Williamson

ALWAYS
LISTEN TO
YOUR HEART

THE BEST DREAMS
HAPPEN WHEN
YOU'RE AWAKE.

Cherie Gilderbloom

I'D RATHER REGRET THE
THINGS I'VE DONE THAN
REGRET THE THINGS
I HAVEN'T DONE.

Lucille Ball

REMEMBER:
HARD TIMES
WILL MAKE YOU
STRONGER

THE DISTANCE IS NOTHING; IT IS ONLY THE FIRST STEP THAT COSTS.

Marie Anne de Vichy-Chamrond

HOW WONDERFUL IT
IS THAT NOBODY NEED
WAIT A SINGLE MOMENT
BEFORE STARTING TO
IMPROVE THE WORLD.

Anne Frank

A WISE MAN WILL MAKE MORE OPPORTUNITIES THAN HE FINDS.

Francis Bacon

WE LIVE IN DEEDS,
NOT YEARS;
IN THOUGHTS,
NOT BREATHS;
IN FEELINGS, NOT IN
FIGURES ON A DIAL.

Philip James Bailey

SLOW
PROGRESS
IS BETTER
THAN NO
PROGRESS

LIFE MOVES ON.
AND SO SHOULD WE.

Spencer Johnson

LIFE IS WAY TOO
SHORT TO SPEND
ANOTHER DAY AT WAR
WITH YOURSELF.

Ritu Ghatourey

NEVER GIVE
UP WHAT
MAKES YOU
HAPPY

DON'T COUNT THE DAYS; MAKE THE DAYS COUNT.

Muhammad Ali

NOTHING GREAT WAS EVER ACHIEVED WITHOUT ENTHUSIASM.

Ralph Waldo Emerson

PROGRESS IS A NICE
WORD. BUT CHANGE
IS ITS MOTIVATOR.

Robert F. Kennedy

YOU MUST DO THE THING... YOU THINK YOU CANNOT DO.

Eleanor Roosevelt

ONLY WORRY
ABOUT THE
THINGS YOU
CAN CHANGE

IF YOU'RE GOING THROUGH HELL, KEEP GOING.

Winston Churchill

JUST WHEN THE
CATERPILLAR
THOUGHT THE
WORLD WAS OVER,
IT BECAME
A BUTTERFLY.

English proverb

COLLECT
MOMENTS,
NOT THINGS

IF YOU WANT TO ACHIEVE
GREATNESS, STOP ASKING
FOR PERMISSION.

Anonymous

EVERYTHING THAT IS
REALLY GREAT AND
INSPIRING IS CREATED
BY THE INDIVIDUAL
WHO CAN LABOUR
IN FREEDOM.

Albert Einstein

MOTIVATION IS WHAT
GETS YOU STARTED.
HABIT IS WHAT
KEEPS YOU GOING.

Jim Ryun

EVEN IF YOU FALL ON
YOUR FACE, YOU'RE
STILL MOVING FORWARD.

Robert C. Gallagher

GO WHERE
YOU'RE
CELEBRATED, NOT
WHERE YOU'RE
TOLERATED

MAKE THE MOST OF
YOURSELF, FOR THAT IS
ALL THERE IS OF YOU.

Ralph Waldo Emerson

ONCE YOU CHOOSE
HOPE, ANYTHING'S
POSSIBLE.

Christopher Reeve

INDULGE
YOURSELF

EVERY MORNING
IS A CHANCE AT
A NEW DAY.

Marjorie Pay Hinckley

TURN YOUR FACE
TO THE SUN AND
THE SHADOWS FALL
BEHIND YOU.

Maori proverb

NORMALITY IS A PAVED
ROAD: IT'S COMFORTABLE
TO WALK, BUT NO
FLOWERS GROW ON IT.

Vincent Van Gogh

HARD WORK BEATS TALENT WHEN TALENT DOESN'T WORK HARD.

Tim Notke

DO WHAT
MAKES YOU
FEEL GOOD

LIFE ISN'T ABOUT
WAITING FOR THE
STORM TO PASS, IT'S
ABOUT LEARNING TO
DANCE IN THE RAIN.

Vivian Greene

EVERY ACCOMPLISHMENT
STARTS WITH THE
DECISION TO TRY.

Gail Devers

IT'S TIME
TO SHOW
THE WORLD
WHAT YOU'RE
MADE OF

YOU'LL MISS THE BEST
THINGS IF YOU KEEP
YOUR EYES SHUT.

Dr Seuss

THERE IS A DESIRE DEEP
WITHIN THE SOUL WHICH
DRIVES MAN FROM THE
SEEN TO THE UNSEEN.

Kahlil Gibran

TO TRAVEL HOPEFULLY
IS A BETTER THING
THAN TO ARRIVE.

Robert Louis Stevenson

IT IS IMPOSSIBLE TO
LIVE WITHOUT FAILING
AT SOMETHING.

J. K. Rowling

LOVE
WHO YOU
ARE

WHEREVER YOU ARE, BE ALL THERE.

Jim Elliot

IMAGINATION IS
MORE IMPORTANT
THAN KNOWLEDGE.
FOR KNOWLEDGE IS
LIMITED, WHEREAS
IMAGINATION EMBRACES
THE ENTIRE WORLD.

Albert Einstein

YOU ARE
THE HERO
OF YOUR
OWN STORY

KNOWING YOURSELF
IS THE BEGINNING
OF ALL WISDOM.

Aristotle

THERE IS NO REASON
NOT TO FOLLOW
YOUR HEART.

Steve Jobs

DO WHAT YOU CAN,
WITH WHAT YOU'VE
GOT, WHERE YOU ARE.

Theodore Roosevelt

STOP CHASING THE
MONEY, AND START
CHASING THE PASSION.

Tony Hsieh

IF YOU
NEVER TRY,
YOU'LL
NEVER KNOW

AT THE END OF THE
DAY, LET THERE
BE NO EXCUSES,
NO EXPLANATIONS,
NO REGRETS.

Steve Maraboli

A YEAR FROM NOW
YOU MAY WISH YOU
HAD STARTED TODAY.

Karen Lamb

YOUR LIFE
IS A SONG;
MAKE SURE
SOMEONE
HEARS IT

YOU CAN'T START
THE NEXT CHAPTER OF
YOUR LIFE IF YOU KEEP
RE-READING THE
LAST ONE.

Anonymous

THINGS DON'T
HAPPEN, THEY ARE
MADE TO HAPPEN.

John F. Kennedy

EVEN IF YOU'RE ON THE
RIGHT TRACK, YOU'LL
GET RUN OVER IF YOU
JUST SIT THERE.

Will Rogers

WHAT WE FEAR DOING
MOST IS USUALLY WHAT
WE MOST NEED TO DO.

Tim Ferriss

LIFE BEGINS
WHEN YOU DO

TOUGH TIMES NEVER LAST, BUT TOUGH PEOPLE DO!

Robert H. Schuller

WHO SEEKS
SHALL FIND.

Sophocles

NOW IS THE
BEST TIME
TO TRY
SOMETHING
NEW

WITH CONFIDENCE YOU HAVE WON EVEN BEFORE YOU HAVE STARTED.

Marcus Garvey

THE SOUL OF A
JOURNEY IS LIBERTY,
PERFECT LIBERTY, TO
THINK, FEEL, DO JUST
AS ONE PLEASES.

William Hazlitt

LIVE EACH DAY AS IF YOUR LIFE HAD JUST BEGUN.

Johann Wolfgang von Goethe

WHEN YOU ARISE
IN THE MORNING,
THINK OF WHAT A
PRECIOUS PRIVILEGE
IT IS TO BE ALIVE — TO
BREATHE, TO THINK,
TO ENJOY, TO LOVE.

Marcus Aurelius

HAVE FAITH
AND BELIEVE
IN YOURSELF

If you're interested in finding out more about our books, find us on Facebook at **Summersdale Publishers** and follow us on Twitter at **@Summersdale**.

www.summersdale.com